THE UNAUTHORIZED BIOGRAPHY

SCOOP!

ISSUE #7

TikTok Stars

by C. D. Bangs

Grosset & Dunlap

GROSSET & DUNLAP
An Imprint of Penguin Random House LLC, New York

Illustrations by Becky James

Photo credits: cover: (Baby Ariel) Amy Sussman/Staff/Getty Images Entertainment/ Getty Images North America; (Addison Rae) Jon Kopaloff/Stringer/Getty Images Entertainment/Getty Images North America; (Chase Hudson) Araya Diaz/Stringer/ Getty Images Entertainment/Getty Images North America; (Charli D'Amelio and Dixie D'Amelio) Monica Schipper/Stringer/Getty Images Entertainment/ Getty Images North America

Visit us online at www.penguinrandomhouse.com.

ISBN 9780593224984   10 9 8 7 6 5 4 3 2 1

TABLE OF CONTENTS

. . . .

CHAPTER 1

THE BEGINNINGS

*A*re you on TikTok? Of course you are! Who *isn't* on TikTok these days? The app has exploded over the past few years, and now major celebs like Lizzo, Cardi B, and Post Malone count themselves as users! But OG TikTok fans know that it wasn't always this way. It's only in the past year or so that the app has gone truly mainstream. In fact, in early 2019 CNN reported that it hit over one billion global users.

> Here's the **SCOOP!** TikTok was released in 2017, and by 2019 it was the seventh most downloaded app of the decade. That's a meteoric rise in two years!

TikTok's true cultural impact became super clear in the beginning of 2020. During Super Bowl LIV in February, Sabra Hummus aired an ad featuring a variety of pop culture figures, including several big TikTok names—dancer Charli D'Amelio, Brittany Tomlinson aka Kombucha Girl, and Zach King, the magician. TikTok even aired its own commercial for the app, and Justin Bieber announced a paid partnership with Chipotle that saw various influencers like David Dobrik making TikToks during the game itself to Justin's latest song, "Yummy."

The day after the Super Bowl, the Iowa Democratic caucus was taking place. The Iowa caucus marks the beginning of the US presidential election season. It's a big deal. And TikTok recognized the opportunity, which led to another huge TikTok moment: Buzzfeed announced they were hiring three "teen ambassadors" to create TikTok news content about the election. This was a *paid gig*, too. Paid to make TikToks! Can you imagine? Sounds like a dream job to us!

All this goes to show that the power of TikTok is only increasing. Brands are constantly looking for where consumers are, and Gen Z has proven to be super unique compared to generations before. Thanks to access to the internet, and the sheer amount of content on it, it's been tricky for brands to find out the best way to market to consumers. TikTok presents an obvious major platform that tons of Gen Z'ers use daily.

Buzzfeed has always been on the pulse of youth culture, but between that and the *Washington Post*'s TikTok accounts, there's a clear sign that news organizations are trying to find ways to not only get the youth aware of the news, journalism, and politics, but even to get them involved!

Of course, it wasn't always this way. TikTok started out way smaller. It was created by the Chinese company ByteDance, which also made Douyin, the Chinese version of the app.

Here's the SCOOP! Lots of apps and social media websites have different versions in China due to the Chinese government's censorship restrictions, which limit what Chinese citizens can access and post on the internet. Since those restrictions don't exist outside of China, ByteDance decided to make a separate app for the international market that wasn't beholden to those same standards. That's TikTok!

Douyin was created in 2016, and quickly became a major deal in China. TikTok was launched by September of the next year. However, in the United States there was already a big-time lip-syncing app that was super popular, called Musical.ly. Sensing an opportunity to capitalize, ByteDance bought Musical.ly for a billion dollars (Yes, you read that right! A *billion*.) and purchased the app with TikTok in November 2017. That's when TikTok started to go supernova. Suddenly, the big names of Musical.ly were also the big names on TikTok, and new users started joining in daily. By January 2018 it was one of the most downloaded apps in the country, and new TikTok stars and content creators were going viral across the platform, gaining major traction.

If other social media platforms like Twitter, Instagram, Vine, and YouTube are any indication, then it's clear that the rising TikTok stars are going to be the mainstream media darlings of tomorrow.

Dancers, actors, cosplayers, comedians, makeup artists, and singers have all embraced the platform, and some of them are already getting huge in major ways. Just before she starred in the Super Bowl commercial of the year, then-fifteen-year-old dancer and creator Charli D'Amelio, her sister, Dixie, and their parents signed with major Hollywood talent agency UTA. UTA plans to take the D'Amelio family big places with new digital content, live touring, and even book and TV deals! Whoa! It seems like soon enough, Charli and Dixie will be more than just TikTok stars.

Here's the SCOOP! At the time of this writing, Charli has just over fifty-three million followers on TikTok. But according to *The Hollywood Reporter*, she's adding as many as 200,000 new followers a day— that's crazy fast growth! By the time you're reading this, she's probably got way more. Check it out!

But wait . . . let's back up. It's one thing to go from TikTok star to mainstream star. It's a whole other thing to get big on the platform to begin with. And there are so many ways to do it! Different creator types find different audiences, and each day new breakthrough people are becoming the next hot TikTokers. Let's take a look at the types of content creators, and some of the biggest names out there to see how they got big!

STARS WHO STARTED OUT ON SOCIAL MEDIA

1. Logan Paul might be known now for his popular and controversial YouTube channel, but what platform did the comedy sketches that helped propel him to stardom appear on?

   A. VINE
   B. MUSICAL.LY
   C. INSTAGRAM
   D. REDDIT

2. Lots of popular singers got their start by posting songs on YouTube. Which one of these stars did not start out on YouTube?

   A. ED SHEERAN
   B. JUSTIN BIEBER
   C. 5 SECONDS OF SUMMER
   D. DRAKE

3. Jacob Sartorius got his music career started by posting to Musical.ly and Vine. Which other superstar got famous posting six-second covers on Vine?

A. LEWIS CAPALDI
B. FRANK OCEAN
C. SHAWN MENDES
D. KHALID

4. SoundCloud has been a fantastic platform for getting new music by young musicians out into the world. Which one of these singers did not find initial success via SoundCloud?

A. HALSEY
B. ARIANA GRANDE
C. BILLIE EILISH
D. CHANCE THE RAPPER

5. Charlie Puth owes a lot to YouTube; his record deal came after a video of him singing a song by which superstar went viral?

A. BEYONCÉ
B. ED SHEERAN
C. ADELE
D. BRUNO MARS

6. John Green is a pretty famous YA author, but before he was a household name, he ran a YouTube channel with his brother—what was it called?

A. VLOGBROTHERS
B. HANK AND JOHN'S YOUTUBE
C. LONG DISTANCE
D. BROTHER TALK

7. Jeffree Star has a makeup empire and a massive YouTube presence. But he first rose to viral fame on this now defunct social media site.

A. FRIEND FEED
B. FORMSPRING
C. MYSPACE
D. FLICKR

8. David Dobrik is huge on YouTube. But which came first for him—his YouTube channel or his Vine account?

A. YOUTUBE

B. VINE

6. Before Lily Singh got her own late-night TV show, she was best known for YouTubing under what username?

A. LONLEYGIRL16

B. IISUPERWOMANII

C. UNICORN

D. RAINBOW GIRL

10. Everyone knows Justin Bieber started on YouTube. But what man, who later had major a public beef with Taylor Swift, discovered him?

A. JOHN MAYER
B. KANYE WEST
C. SCOOTER BRAUN
D. CALVIN HARRIS

How'd you do?
Check your answers
on page 95!

CHAPTER 2

THE MANY DIFFERENT TYPES OF TIKTOKERS

Obviously everyone on TikTok is aiming to get to the *For You* page so they can gain more followers. But people take different approaches and create different types of channels to get there. Let's take a look at some of the core types of TikTokers and what some of the biggest names in those categories are!

The Singers.

Musical.ly was known for lip-syncing videos, but when it merged with TikTok it became obvious that there was some real talent on the platform—TikTok is now filled with super amazing singers. While some people post original content, a lot of people also sing covers or mashups. Big names from Musical.ly, like Loren Gray, Baby Ariel, and Jacob Sartorius, count in the singers group—we'll talk more about them and their rise to fame in a minute. Other big singers include Jeven Reliford, whose videos have gotten him more than three million subscribers.

The Dancers.

Here's where Charli made her claim to fame! One of TikTok's biggest trends is dance: simple movements set to songs that people redo for themselves. Sometimes these are super silly, like the trend for Miley Cyrus's old hit "See You Again." And sometimes they're more technical and difficult, like the Renegade dance challenge, set to Atlanta rapper K Camp's song "Lottery." The Renegade dance challenge was so big that even Lizzo and Millie Bobby Brown were doing it!

The Comedians.

These are the people who would have been huge on Vine (RIP). They know how to use a time limit to their advantage to get a big belly laugh out of someone. Quick thinking, good timing, and lots of charisma give these performers huge crossover viral appeal. Take Brittany Tomlinson (aka Brittany Broski aka Kombucha Girl), whose reaction to drinking kombucha went viral not only on TikTok, but also on Twitter, where it became a super popular reaction GIF.

There's also a ton of crossover between big TikTokers and popular YouTubers and Viners in this category. It should surprise no one that David Dobrik is huge on TikTok, where he has just over twelve million followers—close but not quite as many as his YouTube following of 16.4 million. Similarly, magician Zach King had a following on Vine and YouTube, but he's seen huge success on TikTok, where he has more than thirty-seven million followers.

Here's the **SCOOP!** Brittany told *TIME* magazine that going viral lost her her day job, but given that she now hangs out with stars like Trixie Mattel in sunny LA, we think she may be better off without it!

The Makeup Artists.

While it's no question that YouTube has been the top platform for makeup artists in the past decade (hello to Jeffree Star and James Charles and Manny MUA and Tati Westbrook and gosh, we could go on . . .), TikTok is seeing its own success for the makeup inclined. Makeup trends even have their own memes and challenges, just like dancers! Some true talent has emerged, like Abby Roberts, aka abbyrartistry, and her sister Charlotte, who post beauty and costume makeup transformations. There are also people who do more costume makeup, like the team at Infernum Asylum, who create spooky high-concept videos based on demon characters.

Here's the **SCOOP!** YouTube beauty guru James Charles is on TikTok now, where he posts looks and even participates in memes, as are Manny MUA and Patrick Starrr; even *Elle* magazine is asking if TikTok is the new space for the beauty influencer. YouTube better watch its back!

The Fashionistas.

These are the trendsetters who set new style standards. You know the types. The preppy VSCO girls wear scrunchies, oversized T-shirts, and are always seen with Hydro Flasks; the e-boys and e-girls have their dyed hair, piercings, and goth/ alternative wardrobe; and the kawaii kids rock their anime-inspired outfits and pastel palettes. TikTok has even caused some older fashion trends to resurge, like the early 2000s scene kid look and the '90s grunge aesthetic. Lots of fashionistas also cross over with other types of

TikTokers, like Noen Eubanks, who posts comedy videos to his 10.4 million followers while also repping the e-boy style with French fashion brand Celine. Plus, tons of old-school fashion bloggers are on the platform now, like Brittany Xavier, who regularly posts "outfits of the week" videos to her half a million followers.

These are just some of the big types—there are also tons of popular cosplayers, meme accounts, and just regular celebrities on the app like Will Smith, The Rock, Lizzo, and Justin Bieber. But the truth is that the most successful people on TikTok find a target audience and make content directly for them. Popular TikToker Chase Hudson told the *New York Times* that it helps to have talent, looks, and to be a bit weird! "The weird people get the furthest on the internet." Let's take a look into who some of these popular weirdos are.

But first, Scoop! Quiz time!

WHO SHOULD *YOU* COLLAB WITH?

1. On a Saturday night, you'd most enjoy:

    A. HITTING THE DANCE FLOOR
    B. ALL-NIGHT KARAOKE
    C. MOVIE NIGHT WITH YOUR BESTIES
    D. A BIT OF ALONE TIME

2. Your favorite school subject is:

    A. GYM
    B. MUSIC
    C. ENGLISH
    D. ART

3. You consider your personal style:

A. SUPER TRENDY. YOU'RE ALWAYS ON THE PULSE.

B. COMFY BUT CUTE. YOU SHOULDN'T HAVE TO SACRIFICE EITHER STYLE OR SUBSTANCE.

C. COMPLETELY LAID BACK. YOU'RE NOT SUPER INTO FASHION.

D. A LITTLE WEIRD AND EDGY. YOU'RE AHEAD OF THE TRENDS AND FUTURISTIC.

4. Your favorite genre of movie is:

A. ROM-COMS

B. DRAMAS

C. COMEDIES

D. HORROR

5. Pick a song to set your collab TikTok to!

A. "SAY SO" BY DOJA CAT

B. "WALLS COULD TALK" BY HALSEY

C. "OTHERSIDE" BY PERFUME GENIUS

D. "WAIT A MINUTE!" BY WILLOW

How'd you do?

If you got mostly A's . . . you're a dance fanatic! Call Charli stat; she and you can choreograph a brand-new dance that will sweep the nation!

If you got mostly B's . . . you're a soulful singer! You and Baby Ariel should absolutely do a music vid together. Who's got harmony?

If you got mostly C's . . . you're the comedian in your group! You and Brittany Broski should throw some filters on and goof off.

If you got mostly D's . . . you're the makeup artist! Call Abby Roberts right now and compare your palettes!

HERE'S THE SCOOP!

ON RENEGADE!

Although Charli has been deemed the "CEO" of the Renegade for popularizing it, the dance was originally created by fourteen-year-old Jalaiah Harmon, who posted it on her Instagram. Then it migrated over to TikTok, where it blew up into the viral sensation it is today. Jalaiah picked K Camp's song partially because she's from the Atlanta area herself, and K Camp later thanked her personally for helping his song become a major hit. The *New York Times* profiled Jalaiah in early 2020; after that, Charli invited her to collab on her channel! A bunch of TikTok celebs, including Charli, were invited to the NBA All-Star Game in Chicago, and Jalaiah was able to perform the Renegade in front of a live studio audience. And *then* to top it all off, Michelle Obama even shouted her out for her amazing job, and the next week she appeared on *The Ellen Degeneres Show*! Now she posts new dances to her nearly two million followers on TikTok as @jalaiahharmon. Go Jalaiah!

Charli is obviously one of the bigger dancers on the platform, but there are also other great stars, like the Lopez brothers, Tony and Ondreaz; and Awez Darbar, who boasts more than twenty-three million users on the platform.

CHAPTER 3

THE MUSICAL.LY STARS

*Y*ou can't chat TikTok without getting into Musical.ly! Musical.ly was the OG TikTok, and a lot of the hottest TikTok users are actually originally Musical.ly people! Take Loren Gray— one of the single most followed people on TikTok with more than forty-one million followers. She actually started on Musical.ly back in 2015, when she was in sixth grade. She gained a major following there, which moved over to TikTok when the two apps merged.

Here's the **SCOOP!** Loren says that she got bullied when she gained a big following on Musical.ly, and that it led to her deciding to leave school. But now she has millions of followers, a record deal, more music singles, and two Teen Choice Award noms, which we're pretty sure counts as taking your haters to the bank.

★ Loren Gray: The Superstar ★

Loren Gray was born on April 19, 2002, in Pottstown, Pennsylvania. After hitting it big online, Loren moved to LA to get her singing career off the ground. Moving to LA is a major influencer move—not only is the film and TV industry largely out there, but so are tons of music and talent agents. Loren is a social media *genius*. Not only does she have her giant TikTok and YouTube presences, but she also has six Instagrams, including two professional accounts and two accounts for her super-adorable dogs. Her Insta has more than eighteen million followers, and her YouTube has over 3.5 million subscribers, making her one of the biggest breakout social media stars of her generation. Even OG "it girl" Paris Hilton follows her on Insta!

Loren signed a record deal with Virgin Records in March 2018. That's a month before she turned sixteen. In other words, she had a record deal before she even had a driver's license! Her first single, "My Story," came out that August. Although the song didn't chart in the United States, the lyric video does have more than eight million views, proving that Loren's fans are online and loving her stuff! Since then, she's released more singles—her latest, "Can't Do It," featured the rapper Saweetie.

SCOOP! FACT:

Loren scored her first hit in 2019 collaborating with DJ duo Lost Kings on "Anti-Everything," which made the US dance charts. Go Loren!

Loren Gray isn't the only big TikTok name who started out early . . .

Baby Ariel: The Cool Girl

So did Baby Ariel, who now has more than thirty million TikTok followers. Baby Ariel, who was born November 22, 2000, in Pembroke Pines, Florida, joined Musical.ly in 2015. Her quirky lip-syncing style got her super popular, super fast—she was one of the top people on the platform before the year was even over.

Like Loren, Baby Ariel has since gone into music—she signed a record deal in 2016 and released her first single, "Aww," in 2017. She also appeared on the cover of *Billboard* magazine with fellow Musical.ly star Jacob Sartorius in 2016—who we'll be talking about in a minute! Since "Aww" she's released five more singles, including "Perf." The "Perf" music video has more than thirty-three million views—no small feat!

She's also won two Choice Muser Teen Choice awards (an award specifically for Musical.ly users), in 2016 and 2017—beating Jacob Sartorius both times and Loren Gray in 2016! Does that make her the official winner of the battle of the Musical.ly stars?

Here's the **SCOOP!** Choice Muser was a Teen Choice Award category from 2016 to 2018—the 2018 Teen Choice Awards aired just weeks after Musical.ly merged with TikTok! In the 2019 Teen Choice Awards there was no specific TikTok category— but we'd bet good money one might appear in 2020!

More recently, Ariel has gotten into acting. In 2018 she starred in the Brat web series *Baby Doll Records*. She played Dru, a girl ambitious about her dreams (if not her schoolwork) who starts a record company with some friends but struggles to balance it with her day-to-day responsibilities. She also starred in the 2019 made-for-TV Nickelodeon movie *Bixler High Private Eye* alongside *Harvey Danger* star Jace Norman—and she did a guest spot on a *Harvey Danger* episode that year, too! In February 2020, she starred in *Zombies 2* on the Disney Channel, and was featured on the soundtrack. Ahead of the movie release, her song "The New Kid in Town" premiered on the DisneyMusicVEVO YouTube channel. And, perhaps channeling her TikTok expertise, the music video featured a cute, super-easy-to-learn dance! Can we say "next big thing?"

Baby Ariel spends her time on TikTok lip-syncing, dancing, and generally goofing around. She's got a super great sense of humor that's obvious in all her work—in the "Perf" music video she dates a mannequin, and even has to shove it into a car at one point! It's peak physical comedy. But she's also got a serious side! Way back in 2015 she launched an anti-bullying campaign, #ArielMovement, which got huge traction and support on the net. And in 2015, she was only, well, fifteen!

Ariel and Loren are huge deals, of course, but we

can't talk about Musical.ly without talking about the one and only Jacob Sartorius!

Jacob Sartorius: The Heartthrob

Jacob Sartorius was born in Tulsa, Oklahoma, in 2002. Perhaps the biggest crossover star Musical.ly ever had, Jacob signed with T3 Records in 2016 and released his first single, "Sweatshirt," that year. "Sweatshirt" hit the Top 100 chart at number ninety, and also charted in Canada. He also released a full extended play, *The Last Text*, in 2017, and went on a world tour to promote it. His second single, "Hit or Miss," came from that EP and saw some pretty good success—the music video has more than sixty-seven million views on YouTube, and the single charted at seventy-two in the United States, making it his most successful single to date! The whole EP was a success, hitting the *Billboard* 200 chart in the United States. The EP even hit international charts in Australia,

Ireland, Scotland, Canada, and New Zealand.

In 2017, Jacob hopped from T3 to major player RCA Records, and released his major label debut, *Left Me Hangin'*. He's released two more EPs since then, 2018's *Better with You* and 2019's *Where Have You Been?*

Jacob is still huge on TikTok, with more than twenty-two million followers.

Here's the SCOOP! Jacob went viral from his very first video, a Vine speaking out against bullying that he posted in 2014 at the age of eleven.

Like Baby Ariel and Loren, Jacob has also brought activism into his public life and image. In 2018, he spoke at the LA branch of the March for Our Lives, organized by survivors of the Parkland school shooting in Florida.

Jacob's personal life may have overtaken his TikTok one. He might be most famous now for his relationship with *Stranger Things* star Millie Bobby Brown, whom he started dating in 2018. The two had a tumultuous relationship, breaking up before the end of the year and then reuniting in early 2019, but they seem to be officially split now. Still, there's no denying that Jacob is a major name in the Gen Z celeb space, and we expect his star to continue to rise!

Another pair of TikTok stars who started out on Musical.ly and are now making waves in the music industry are . . . *drumroll, please . . .*

★ Cash and Mav: The Up-and-Comers ★

Cash and Maverick Baker. Cash boasts an impressive 24.5 million followers, and Maverick has 12.3 million. They also have a joint TikTok, @cashandmav, that has over seven million followers—that's a total of 43.8 million followers across all their TikTok accounts. Not too shabby!

Although they may look like twins, don't be fooled—the Baker brothers are actually three years apart! Older bro Maverick was born on December 13, 2000, and Cash was born on March 5, 2003. A Sagittarius and a Pisces? Now that's an interesting duo! The brothers were born and raised in Henryetta, Oklahoma, a town of fewer than six thousand people.

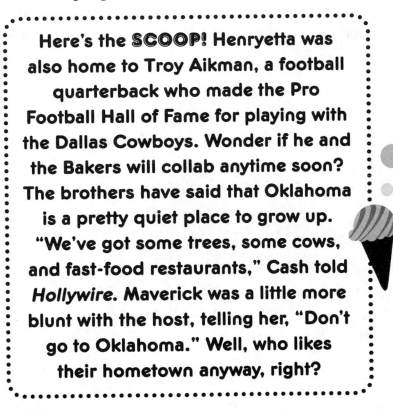

Here's the **SCOOP!** Henryetta was also home to Troy Aikman, a football quarterback who made the Pro Football Hall of Fame for playing with the Dallas Cowboys. Wonder if he and the Bakers will collab anytime soon? The brothers have said that Oklahoma is a pretty quiet place to grow up. "We've got some trees, some cows, and fast-food restaurants," Cash told *Hollywire*. Maverick was a little more blunt with the host, telling her, "Don't go to Oklahoma." Well, who likes their hometown anyway, right?

Believe it or not, Cash and Maverick actually aren't the first famous people in their family! Their older sister, Lani Lynn Baker, is a social media influencer in her own right, with half a million Instagram followers. She's also a model and an actress—so it's a pretty successful family!

While their sister might be a fashionista, Cash and Maverick are slightly more traditional. Maverick told *Hollywire* his favorite fashion trend was nerd chic. "This kid, if he could, he would dress in a bow tie and suspenders and his shirt tucked in *every day*," Cash said. As for Cash, well, he's not big into the fashion scene either. Apparently, he'd been wearing the shirt he wore to that interview for four days. Although he did say he washed it, which we guess makes it fair game.

Although Cash and Maverick aren't huge like Baby Ariel, Loren Gray, or Jacob yet, they're absolutely on their way! They released their first music video, "Whatever It Takes," on April 14, 2019, and by early 2020 it had more than thirty-two million views on YouTube. Since then, they've released four other songs with accompanying YouTube videos: "Queen," "Good Thing," "All My Life," and "Space Cowboy." All those were released in 2019, leading up to their early 2020 announcement that they were going on a national tour! Unfortunately, due to the coronavirus pandemic, the Elevation Tour was cancelled. Despite the cancellation, this is an impressive accomplishment for a pair with no official album yet. Although they did tease an EP around the corner!

But we know why you're really here—to get the SCOOP! Duh. So are the brothers dating anyone? In October 2019, both brothers told *Hollywire* they were single—Cash even spilled that he'd never had an official girlfriend before! But they did share some ideal relationship goals. Maverick likes a kind girl. "Be nice, be genuine," he said. As for Cash, he didn't have too many specifics, but he did spill his celebrity crush . . . none other than Ariana Grande herself!

The brothers also revealed some super fun

facts to Famous Birthdays in a game of "Who's More Likely?" Maverick hates scary movies. "I'll walk out," he said. While Cash is most likely to break into laugher during a serious moment. In fact, Cash seems to be the funny one of the duo. Each brother also said he was more likely to be a stand-up comedian. Maverick, meanwhile, is the sensitive one, with both brothers saying he was more likely to get his heart broken and more likely to cry during a movie.

It really seems like Cash and Maverick are about to break big into the music scene. In February 2020 the brothers signed on with management company Shots Studios, who also manage Vine stars Lele Pons and Rudy Mancuso! Shots Studios plans to help the brothers develop on other platforms like YouTube, as well as create new content like podcasts and further their musical ambitions. But Cash and Maverick are doing pretty alright for themselves already, selling a full line of merch on their website—including plushies of themselves. Innovative!

The brothers are super focused on their music careers, but their personal TikToks are a space for them to relax and have fun. Most of their videos are them dancing around and goofing off with each other or their friends—including Mychael @mychaelade, who has more than eight million followers himself!

These aren't the only stars to break from Musical.ly to TikTok. There's also Danielle Cohn, who was one of the first people to surpass ten million followers on Musical.ly and now has more than sixteen million followers on TikTok. Not to mention Kristen Hanchner, who currently has more than twenty-three million TikTok followers and also works with Logan Paul at Team 10. But Loren, Baby Ariel, Jacob, and Cash and Maverick are special because they've shown the ability to cross over from social media stardom to fame in other areas. They've also shown real staying power! It goes to show if you have something cool and fun you can do, you shouldn't be afraid to bring it to the world!

But before we go any further about TikTok stars, let's take a quick break and focus on another star . . . you!

FIVE QUICK TIPS TO STEP UP
YOUR LIP-SYNC SKILLS!

Lip-syncing was the entire point of Musical.ly, and it has continued to be a huge part of TikTok. Almost every huge TikTok star lip–syncs. Here are some tips to make your lip-sync game stellar.

1

Spend some time memorizing the audio. This seems obvious, but we don't just mean the words. Note where the original song or speaker pauses for breath, the changes in their tone or pitch, and any time they might slip, stutter, or otherwise take an odd break.

2

Practice in front of a mirror. Once you've memorized the audio, spend some time in front of the mirror watching yourself say the words. What looks odd? Where are you messing up the words? Seeing yourself do it for a bit will really help you fine-tune any problem areas.

3

Speak out loud when you record. The best way to make it look like you're really talking is to really talk! Pop stars perfected this tactic; while most music videos are dubbed over by the studio track, lots of pop stars sing live during the recording to make sure their mouth moves as naturally as possible. Since you'll be dubbing over what you're saying, no one will hear what you're really saying anyway!

4

Exaggerate your lips. If you watch yourself speak, you'll probably notice that your mouth doesn't move too much. But on video, it helps to make everything a little bit more outsized so you can really see it clearly. Move your lips more than you might naturally when you talk—overemphasize and articulate—and you'll look a lot larger and clearer on camera.

5

Move a little. Very few people sit completely still when they talk. Don't be afraid to add some natural movement of your head or hands for emphasis. It adds to the realism!

CHAPTER 4

CHARLI D'AMELIO AND HYPE HOUSE

*I*f you're on TikTok, you know about Charli. Her videos are *everywhere*. She starts dance trends and people love to duet and contribute their own versions of her videos! But just who *is* Charli?

 Charli: The Breakout Star

Charli was born on May 1, 2004, in Norwalk, Connecticut, to Marc and Heidi D'Amelio. She has one sister, Dixie, who's nineteen and also major on TikTok—odds are you've seen her videos floating around the *For You* page, or you've seen one of her many collabs with her sister. Charli joined TikTok in the summer of 2019 and by the end of the year was one of the biggest homegrown stars on the platform, a seriously wild exponential growth.

Charli's status as one of TikTok's first homegrown stars made her a big name both on and off the platform, but she's stayed humble with her newfound fame. Even she admits she doesn't get the hype about herself. In late 2019, she told *MEL* magazine, "I wish I could give everyone an explanation as to what happened, but I have no idea. I'm just doing what I do every day and posting it."

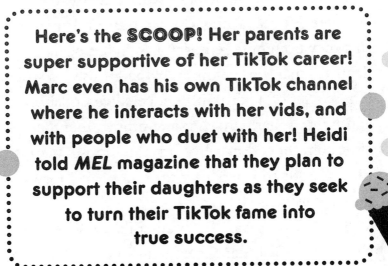

Here's the SCOOP! Her parents are super supportive of her TikTok career! Marc even has his own TikTok channel where he interacts with her vids, and with people who duet with her! Heidi told *MEL* magazine that they plan to support their daughters as they seek to turn their TikTok fame into true success.

It's true that TikTok can make an accidental celebrity out of almost anyone. Part of Charli's major success is also, unfortunately, the people who hate-consume her content. Hate-watching is a major part of TikTok, and Charli says that the negativity can get gross and overwhelming. Like Baby Ariel and Loren before her, Charli receives tons of negative comments. But luckily for her, she's also made a tight-knit group of friends on TikTok.

In fact, she and her friends work directly together at Hype House, a huge, super beautiful mansion that they bought together in LA. Like Logan Paul's Team 10 mansion before it, Hype House is a space where a set of TikTok influencers live, collaborate, and work. Charli and Dixie are both members—although they don't live in the house because they're both still finishing up school in Norwalk. So responsible!

Hype House was the brainchild of seventeen-year-old TikTok star Chase Hudson, aka lilhuddy, and Thomas Petrou, who both realized that they would benefit from having a home base to live, work, and create in. They found and bought a house in LA toward the end of 2019 for just that purpose, and invited a ton of their friends to join up. Given how young everyone is, not everyone who is "in" Hype House officially lives there. But they all visit constantly, and you can see the totally stunning property in the background of many of their videos.

 ## Chase: The Cool Kid

Chase was born on May 15, 2002, in Stockton, California. He began making lip-sync and dance videos on TikTok in 2019, and quickly amassed a huge following—as of this writing he has more than seventeen million followers. He didn't start out super popular though—he even told *Entertainment Tonight* that his first TikTok was "horrible." But Chase persevered—in the same interview he said that he always wanted to be famous, and that he kept making videos despite his sisters making fun of him.

SCOOP! FACT:

Like Charli, Chase has supportive parents, who both have rallied behind his TikTok career. But when he was a child, his parents turned down modeling opportunities for his sisters and him because they wanted the kids to have proper schooling—after all, his parents are both teachers! They're now letting him finish school online so he can stay in LA and work on the next steps in his career.

Chase is now popular enough that he's snagged major brand deals, doing sponcon for huge hitters like American Eagle. That makes sense considering he's known for his fashion style—he was one of the first mainstream e-boys! He was a guest on the 2019 Lights Out Tour, which sent tons of social media stars across the country for meet and greets with fans. Other stars on the tour included Cynthia

Parker, Payton Moormeier, Josh Richards, and Anthony Reeves—who would eventually go on to join a different collab house called Sway House.

Chase and Thomas started discussing Hype House in November 2019, and found the actual house super quick, signing a lease in LA just thirteen days after they began planning! Chase told the *New York Times* that he wanted to name it "House of Olympus," but was outvoted when fellow member Alex Warren suggested Hype House. Hype House isn't the only plan Chase has in the pipeline—he told *Entertainment Tonight* that he's working in the music sphere, and that his dream is to be an entrepreneur and start several businesses. So maybe Hype House is just the start of the Chase Hudson empire!

Although Hype House was created largely as a work space, there's tons of other benefits, too. As Charli told the *New York Times*, "The internet can be a little harsh. Everyone here is ready to bring positivity and kindness." There's something super special about sharing a space with your friends, and the support you get there!

Here's the SCOOP! Although Chase and Charli claimed not to be dating in an early January 2020 interview with the *New York Times*, they looked fully coupled up on a trip to Hawaii that month. Later, in February, Chase told *Entertainment Tonight* that the two were avoiding labels and taking it slow, but "we are very exclusive and very into each other." But by April, the two decided they were ultimately better as friends, posting separate Instagrams that they had broken up. Charli wrote, "We are still close friends and I would not change that for anything! I truly have so much love for Chase," while Chase called her an "amazing person." We were personally devastated to see them break up, but we love that they're still friends and are excited to see how both their careers develop!

But luckily love is still in the air in the Hype House! Alex Warren and Kouvr Annon are also members, and they've been dating since 2018. Although Alex also has a big TikTok presence now, with more than seven million followers, he originally got big on YouTube, where he has more than 900K subscribers. These days, you can see him pranking other members of Hype House, or collabing with them on comedy sketches and stunts!

Okay, so a giant LA mansion filled with teens . . . must be a total party house, right? Wrong! The creators who live in Hype House take TikTok seriously, considering it a career or a step toward the future careers they want. In an interview with the *New York Times*, they clarified the Hype House Rules: you can have friends over, but you can't party; if you break something, you have to replace it; and most importantly, to stay in, you have to create at least one video a day.

Of course, that last rule is no problem for Charli and Chase, who regularly put out five to seven videos daily. In fact, one of the big keys to Charli's success is that she'll often post multiple videos of her doing the same dance moves to the same songs. This increases the likelihood of getting those dances moves on the *For You* page, and also means that more people see the moves over and over again, and learn the dances faster. That's how she helps create viral dance trends like the Renegade. By the time you see her doing it for the fourth or fifth time, you know all the moves and want to join in! Thomas told the *New York Times* that he figured at least one hundred videos a day were being made at Hype House. That's truly prolific content creation. But it's not just Charli and Chase who are pumping out videos. The other members are productive creators as well.

So who *are* the other members of Hype House?

★ Thomas Petrou: The Brains ★

First, there's co-founder Thomas Petrou, who used to be affiliated with Logan Paul's Team 10.

Thomas is the oldest member of Hype House at age twenty-one, and is best known for his daily vlogs, which he's been doing for more than five hundred consecutive days. Thomas is often credited as the brains behind Hype House. He pointed out to *Entertainment Tonight* that TikTok is a business opportunity not only for the creators themselves, but for the musicians whose tracks get turned into viral challenges or memes. Thomas said that TikTok is bigger than the radio—and he might be right! Musicians like Conan Gray, Roddy Ricch, Doja Cat, and K Camp have all seen huge chart success after their songs went viral on TikTok.

★ Addison Rae: The Sweetheart ★

Then there's Addison Rae, who, like Charli, mostly posts lip-syncs and dance videos. Addison, whose real last name is Easterling, has more than twenty-seven million followers on the app and has worked with huge stars like Mackenzie Ziegler and James

Charles. She was born on October 6, 2000, in Lafayette, Louisiana, and signed on with talent agency WME in 2020.

SCOOP! FACT:

Addison says she originally downloaded TikTok as a joke, but when her first video went viral she realized the app had potential. "I realized, like, you could actually get somewhere on this app!" she told *Entertainment Tonight*.

Addison does tons of videos with her mom, who's super supportive—and has 3.7 million TikTok followers herself! The video of them dancing to Mariah Carey's "Obsessed" was even liked by the queen diva! Addison told *Entertainment Tonight* she was starstruck by that. "It was like, so crazy," she gushed. That video was the first of Addison's to really go viral, hitting over a million views. Family is really important to Addison, who hopes to eventually use her TikTok career to fully support her family.

★ Avani Gregg: The Style Queen ★

Another big name on the app and in Hype House is Avani Gregg. Avani, who has more than fourteen million followers, is also a dancer like Charli and Addison. Born on November 23, 2002, in Indiana, Avani is currently dating Anthony Reeves, aka luvanthony. Avani considers Charli and Addison among her best friends, and the three often collab and post together as part of the house! Avani's popularity is growing; in 2020 she was even nominated for a Shorty Award for TikToker of the Year, the only member of Hype House to be honored.

★ The Brothers . . . and more! ★

Then there are the brothers . . . the Lopez brothers, that is, Ondreaz and Tony! Also dancers, also mega-popular, they have a combined following of more than nineteen million people! While you can catch them choreographing new moves in the Hype House living room these days, the brothers were raised in Las Vegas, and began their dance careers on Instagram.

SCOOP! FACT:

The Shorty Awards started giving out the TikToker of the Year award in 2019, and started nominating TikTokers in other categories in 2020. The first winner of the TikToker of the Year was . . . a cat! Nala the cat, to be specific, who beat out a stacked category including Nathan Piland, Dominic Toliver, and Awez Darbar. The 2020 TikToker of the Year nominees include Avani Gregg, Brittany Broski, and Howie Mandel!

Avani is also a huge Billie Eilish fan, and loves *The Office*. She told *Hollywire* that she's watched the series all the way through thirty-nine times. Now that's superfan status!

And that's not even all of them, it's just the tip of the iceberg. Other members include Daisy Keech, Calvin Goldby, Ryland Storms, Wyatt Xavier, Patrick Huston, Nick Austin, Connor Yates, Hootie Hurley, and Daisy's dog, Harley. And like other collaborative efforts, they'll likely continue to bring people into the fold.

Hype House received a lot of, well, hype when they first launched. They were profiled in the *New York Times*, which led to tons of other coverage. Chase even cohosted an episode of *Entertainment Tonight* in late February 2020 where he and the rest of the house made appearances and talked about their plans. We can expect to see more big moves from them as they continue to grow!

Okay, so we've established that Hype House is a pretty big deal—it's a super popular collaborative effort. It's also just the first of what will eventually be a big trend of TikTok creators banding together to make mini media companies to promote and create work. In fact, other big houses and efforts are already emerging! Let's chat about an up-and-coming Hype House rival: Sway House!

But first, let's have ourselves a little quiz!

SCOOP! QUIZ

HOW WELL DO *YOU* KNOW VIRAL
⬇ TIKTOK AUDIOS? ⬇

1. mxmtoon released her debut EP to great success in 2018. On TikTok, she might be best known for a song where she's "crying" in this article of clothing.

   A. MOM JEANS
   B. COMBAT BOOTS
   C. PROM DRESS
   D. BEST DRESS

   Hint: It's a remixed verson so Lil Jon is hyping her up in between lines.

2. "Maniac" by this artist went super viral on TikTok thanks to a catchy hook where he sings, "Tell all of your friends that I'm crazy and drive you mad."

   A. CONAN GRAY
   B. CONNOR SMITH
   C. COREY CRAWFORD
   D. CONAN O'BRIEN

   Hint: He was successful before— opening up for Panic! At the Disco in early 2019.

3. Roddy Ricch won a Grammy in early 2020 for a song he did with the late Nipsey Hussle, but his highest charting song was also a TikTok hit thanks to its distinctive intro. What song is it?

A. "LALA SONG"
B. "THE BOX"
C. "DISSOLVE"
D. "VIBEZ"

4. Post Malone had a major hit with "Circles" way before TikTok tweaked it, adding a line from what 2002 film and rocketing it to meme status?

A. *ICE AGE*
B. *TOY STORY*
C. *A BUG'S LIFE*
D. *CARS*

5. Arizona Zervas had major TikTok success with his song "Roxanne," where he laments that the titular girl only wants to do what?

A. SLEEP UNTIL NOON
B. DANCE UNTIL DAWN
C. PARTY ALL NIGHT
D. SING ABOUT IT

6. In a popular TikTok audio, this San Francisco rapper claims that he "sold his soul to the devil for designer."

A. CHANCE THE RAPPER
B. TRAVIS SCOTT
C. 24KGOLDN
D. QUAVO

7. Doja Cat owes a lot of her success to TikTok. Her first viral hit was "Moo," but this song that went viral on the app was her first Top Ten hit.

A. "JUICY"
B. "SAY SO"
C. "TIA TAMERA"
D. "LIKE THAT"

8. TikTok isn't just about new music. Sometimes older songs go mega viral too, like this 1983 hit where the singer claims "he had the strangest dream, I sailed away to China in a little rowboat to find ya."

A. "BREAK MY STRIDE"

B. "MANIAC"

C. "COME SAIL AWAY"

D. "KARMA CHAMELEON"

★ ★ ⭐ ★ ★

9. Similarly, TikTok dance challenges gave a new life to this singer's 2010 hit "Cannibal," where she declares that she'll "eat you up."

A. KATY PERRY

B. NICKI MINAJ

C. LADY GAGA

D. KESHA

10. Not every viral audio is a song! In mid-2020 TikTok MUAs started doing their makeup over audio clips of this *Kid Gorgeous* comedian's stand-up.

A. PETE DAVIDSON
B. KEVIN HART
C. JOHN MULANEY
D. AMY SCHUMER

How'd you do? Check your answers on page 95!

CHAPTER 5

WHO COMES NEXT?

*W*e all know that Hype House got a lot of attention when it was announced! Some of this is due to the sheer popularity of the people involved, but a lot of it is also that it signifies the new era of TikTok as a major social media force and star creator, like YouTube and Vine before it. Not long after Hype House started, TalentX Entertainment, a talent company, announced Sway House—a similar collab house featuring another group of pretty popular TikTokers.

 Anthony Reeves: The Fashion King

Among the first people in Sway House was Anthony Reeves, aka luvanthony, aka Avani

Gregg's boyfriend who has more than seven million followers on TikTok and more than three million on Insta. Talk about a crossover—two collab houses, both alike in dignity!

Anthony was born on November 7, 2001, in Ashland, Kentucky. He started out largely lip-syncing and dancing but has also become known for his style. He's even made several successful videos showing his huge collection of offbeat and designer clothing. Anthony's first big video was a dance he did with fellow star Jaden Hossler, which went viral. Jaden and Anthony have remained close friends. In fact, Jaden is also a founding member of Sway House!

 ## Jaden Hossler: The Jokester

Jaden was born on February 18, 2001, in Chattanooga, Tennessee. He currently has more than four million TikTok followers. Although Jaden's internet presence is mostly goofy, he also has a serious creative side. He's posted videos of himself playing original songs, and in early 2020 teased dropping a full single. With Sway House behind him, Jaden might be making a strong move into music like Loren Gray and Baby Ariel! His videos also occasionally feature his mother, Denae, who's a huge supporter of his career.

Here's the SCOOP! In late 2019, Jaden announced that he was dating Mads Lewis, an Instagram influencer and star of Brat's popular web series *Chicken Girls*. Looks like Charli and Chase might have some cutest couple competition!

★ Kio Cyr: The Charmer ★

Also in Sway House is Kio Cyr. Kio posts tons of videos to his 4.5 million followers. He participates in lots of viral challenges and memes, but also makes POV videos where he plays out various scenarios—like seeing your ex at a party, or getting a new deskmate at school. In early 2020 Kio was included on the Juice Krate Tour, a national tour of social media stars and influencers, including Jeremy Hutchins, Cynthia Parker, and Zachary Smith, aka zsmittty.

Rounding out Sway House are a couple dudes who were famous before TikTok—Instagram star Bryce Hall and YouTuber Nick Bean.

 ## Bryce Hall: The IG King

Bryce, who was born on August 14, 1999, also had a pretty big following of over 30K on Vine before the app shuttered. While he has three million Insta followers, he's surpassed that on TikTok, where he has more than four million followers who log in to see his quirky, relatable comedy videos and dance moves. He also has nearly two million followers on

YouTube now, where you can see him vlog from Sway House itself!

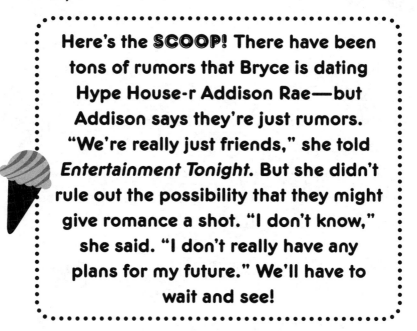

Here's the **SCOOP!** There have been tons of rumors that Bryce is dating Hype House-r Addison Rae—but Addison says they're just rumors. "We're really just friends," she told *Entertainment Tonight.* But she didn't rule out the possibility that they might give romance a shot. "I don't know," she said. "I don't really have any plans for my future." We'll have to wait and see!

★ Nick Bean: The YouTube Star ★

Nick Bean, meanwhile, started out on YouTube, where he has around 1.5 million subscribers. The oldest member of Sway House, he was born on March 13, 1995, in Maiden, North Carolina. Nick was once part of the collaborative YouTube channel Our Journey, which featured some other super familiar names—Loren Gray and Baby Ariel were both on it! Small world!

Here's the SCOOP! Nick had an incredibly impressive YouTube start, gaining more than five thousand followers in the first week of his channel! His TikTok already has 2.1 million followers, too. We wonder how helpful Sway House has been in growing his impressive following!

But you can't talk Sway House boys without bringing up their heaviest hitter . . . the one and only Josh Richards!

 ## Josh Richards: The Heavy Hitter

Josh Richards is a megastar talent with fifteen million followers on TikTok. In fact, Josh is so big on TikTok he has a second, alternate account at uhhhjosh—which has 2.6 million followers! That's a lot of people watching his videos. He's also acted professionally, with roles in the movies *Brother's Keeper* and *Summertime Dropouts*.

In early 2020 Josh announced that he was dating fellow TikTok star Nessa Barrett. The two released a YouTube video detailing the relationship, including the fact that they managed to keep it secret for four months! Nessa is of course most famous for her dancing and lip-syncing videos, which she posts to her more than five million followers. We're total Jessa shippers over here at SCOOP! And we're totally impressed they managed to keep it quiet for so long!

If nothing else, Sway House definitely proves that there's a hunger for collaborative working spaces for TikTok creators. Working together has been a key way influencers that have grown their followings on the platform. Chase fans following Charli, Charli fans following Avani, Avani fans following Anthony . . . the list goes on! Although the boys in Sway House might not be as famous as the Hype House kids, we predict that they're on their way up and that we'll see pretty big things from them soon!

CHAPTER 6

TIKTOK ACTIVISM

*W*e've talked a lot about the ways in which TikTok is super fun, energetic, and hilarious. But TikTok also has a serious side! Most TikTok users are Gen Z and Millennials. And studies are showing that those two generations are more involved in activism and social responsibility than ever. A 2019 survey by Irregular Labs showed that 75 percent of Gen Z respondents cited social activism as extremely important to their identity. And these movements are being seen all over the world, from the Parkland students organizing the March for Our Lives, to Greta Thunberg's climate strike.

As more Zoomers get involved in social movements, more of the content they create revolves around issues they're passionate about! On

TikTok, tons of users create memes about politics and share information for how to be active in one's community. For example, during the coronavirus pandemic in early 2020, a lot of xenophobia and racism toward Chinese people reared its head in the world and in the media. Asian TikTok creators spoke out against this in tons of videos, addressing how harmful the stereotypes were. Buzzfeed even pulled a whole article together covering some of the most popular videos standing up against these harmful stereotypes.

Here's the SCOOP! Lots of people also use TikTok to discuss climate change, and what young people can do to help the environment and to take action to improve the world, both in big ways and in small personal steps. Plus, lots of people made videos encouraging teens to register to vote in 2020 and educating them

about issues that were super relevant in the election, like immigration, women's rights, and LGBTQ rights!

But social activism isn't just limited to videos *on* TikTok. In fact, a lot of users are speaking out about TikTok itself, and the way the platform is run. TikTokers of color have spoken out about how the most popular accounts on the app are overwhelmingly white, and how white creators have an easier time getting onto the *For You* page. In 2020, *ONE Magazine* interviewed several black women TikTokers who said that their comments are often filled with racist remarks. User Bria Jones said, "I think that [not getting on the *For You* page] comes down to people subconsciously not interacting with women of color's content, therefore the algorithm is not feeding you more of that content." There have even been memes outlining the difficulty black creators have getting appreciated. For example, one popular audio mixed Beach Bunny's song "Prom Queen" with

Chalie Boy's "I Look Good," following the first song's request to be a "blue-eyed blondie" with a reassurance that the singer "looks fly" and "looks good." This audio was mostly used by creators of color to speak up against the overwhelmingly white beauty standard that exists in the world, while also hyping themselves.

One of the keys to helping improve diversity on TikTok is simply supporting creators of color. When Jalaiah Harmon told the *New York Times* that she invented the Renegade dance, she was standing up for a long tradition of creators of color seeing their creative work stolen or meme-ified without their consent or any ability to monetize or promote off their work. When she had previously tried to take credit in TikTok comments, she was mostly made fun of or dismissed.

Similar things happen to creators of color, particularly black creators, all the time! Peaches Monroee created a Vine where she referred to her eyebrows as "on fleek," coining a new term for looking good. It went viral, and soon everyone was saying "on fleek," and it began appearing on shirts, bags, and other merch. But Peaches herself struggled to get any credit for the work she'd done to popularize the phrase she made up. More than that, compared to other viral content creators from that year, she barely got any attention at all. The "Damn Daniel" kids were invited on *Ellen*, and were given a free lifetime supply of Vans shoes from the company, even though all they made was one funny video. Similarly, Chewbacca Mom, whose video of herself laughing at a noise-making Chewbacca mask went viral, was able to turn her viral fame into college scholarships for her kids. While those videos were enjoyable and undeniably popular, it's hard to argue they had anywhere near the same cultural impact as the video Peaches made did—and yet, she wasn't invited onto TV or given free products for her work.

Eventually, Peaches was able to rally support thanks to journalists who promoted her cause in *Wired*, *Teen Vogue*, and other outlets, launching a makeup line and even filing to trademark the phrase. Jalaiah almost certainly learned from watching people before her—even though she's only fourteen, she knew it was wrong that she wasn't getting credit for something she invented. That's why it was such a breath of fresh air when the internet largely rallied behind her—everyone from Charli herself to Lizzo and other big celebs were excited for her and invited her into spaces to celebrate her achievements.

All of this has two big takeaways . . .

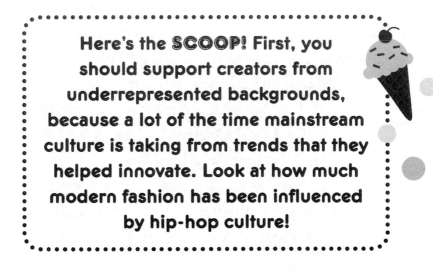

Here's the SCOOP! First, you should support creators from underrepresented backgrounds, because a lot of the time mainstream culture is taking from trends that they helped innovate. Look at how much modern fashion has been influenced by hip-hop culture!

And second, if you see someone stealing content without credit, especially content from creators of color, call it out! Support the original creators! Jalaiah is on TikTok, Dubsmash, YouTube, and Instagram creating awesome new dances every day.

Users have also called out TikTok for homophobia—both in user-created content, and in how the app enforces its own community guidelines. User Mark Pasetsky wrote an article in *Campaign US* complaining about TikTok removing a video of him chastely kissing his male partner on New Year's for "breaking community guidelines." In fact, many LGBTQ creators have stated that pro-LGBTQ content has a high chance of getting flagged and removed. Initially, the app claimed that this was an attempt to curb homophobic bullying in the comments of these videos, but users rightfully pointed out that it appeared to be punishing the poster more than the actual bullies.

Further, there's an interesting political issue with TikTok, namely that it's a Chinese-owned app. China's government censors lots of content on the internet. For instance, China doesn't allow Twitter or Facebook past the country's firewalls. Content that is explicitly critical of the Chinese government is generally a no-go on the Chinese web. But some TikTok users say that criticizing the Chinese government is a no-go on TikTok even for noncitizens. In November 2019, seventeen-year-old Feroza Aziz said she was banned from the app after posting a video criticizing the Chinese internment of Uyghur Muslims. TikTok said she was banned for other reasons, but the story got so much traction it was eventually featured in the *New York Times*.

All of this is pretty heavy stuff, and it can be super disappointing to learn that an app you love has a downside. But there is some good to come from all of this, and that's that you can make a difference! Because Feroza complained about being taken down, TikTok eventually had to reverse the decision to ban her and apologize. While they claimed it was simply human error, the reinstatement of her account is a step in the right direction. And when LGBTQ creators complained about getting censored, TikTok agreed to review their internal policies and try to do better.

What's good about all of this is that as a TikTok user, you have a lot of power to create real change on the app! TikTok needs users to survive, and if enough of them complain about unfair practices, racist algorithms, and broken community guidelines, TikTok will have to listen to them in order to keep their user base happy. So if you see something on TikTok you don't like—a user making cruel comments, videos getting taken down that shouldn't be—make some noise! The power to change the conversation is in your hands. Use it!

FIVE TIPS ON HOW *YOU* CAN MAKE A DIFFERENCE ONLINE!

The first steps to changing the world can be small ones! Here are some super easy ways you can make TikTok safer and more fun for everyone.

Report people who leave derogatory or bullying comments, or who make inappropriate or otherwise cruel videos. Reporting people who create negative content helps get them removed from the site and stops them from spreading that energy to the people they're trying to hurt.

2

Don't leave nasty comments, even if you think no one can see them. Even people with thousands or millions of followers can read your comments, so it's better to keep your meaner thoughts to yourself.

3

Support creators of different races, genders, sexualities, and abilities. Tons of people are out there making great content—seek them out! There's no reason your feed should only be about one type of person.

4

Speak out on other social media if you see something bad happening on TikTok. Notice a creator get banned for posting LGBTQ content? See a video get taken down that you don't think deserved it? Spread the word!

5

Make your own videos about what you're passionate about. If you know a great local charity, hear about a protest you want people to join, or just want to rally some friends to save the turtles, make a video! You never know what might end up going viral on TikTok and changing someone's mind!

CHAPTER 7

THE FUTURE

*T*ikTok is obviously the social media of the minute—but what will happen next? Well, it's hard to say! The internet is a constantly changing and evolving place, and things that are huge one minute are capable of collapsing the next.

TikTok gets tons of comparisons to Vine, the social media video app that shuttered in 2016 at what seemed like the height of its popularity. The story of Vine seems ominous to many people when they discuss the staying power of TikTok. But even though the platform is gone, tons of stars who made their names on Vine are finding mainstream success. The Paul Brothers, Jay Versace, Rudy Mancuso, and King Bach are all still successful, even with Vine itself out of the picture.

Vine's much-hyped successor, Byte, launched in early 2020, and seemed like the first big competitor to come after TikTok. While it remains to be seen exactly how successful Byte will be, its initial launch didn't have a major impact on TikTok uploads or usership. Even if Byte rises, it'll be likely that there will be tons of crossovers with TikTok users trying to find new audiences and promote across both apps, like they already do on Insta, Twitter, and YouTube.

All of this is to say that even if TikTok doesn't make it long into the 2020s, the people who've gotten big on the platform are likely not going anywhere anytime soon. As they grow their platforms online, they're also finding ways to become even bigger names and bigger stars. Charli is obviously leading the charge here. She was one of the most talked about people by the end of 2019, and in early 2020, it felt like she was everywhere! She and Addison Rae made an appearance at the

NBA All-Star Game, and then the next day Charli was seen at Prada during Milan Fashion Week. And while Charli and Prada weren't officially working together, she *did* make a TikTok with the models.

Prada isn't the first big designer brand to invite TikTok stars to its shows. Charli's beau, Chase, and Loren Gray were both invited to the Dolce & Gabbana show in Milan. *The Cut* theorizes that TikTok stars are in the same cultural market that bloggers were in the early 2000s, or that YouTubers were in the 2010s. Having them at your events shows a direct attempt to appeal to a younger market, while also showing that the people running the show know who's cool enough to sit in the front row.

It all goes to show that the odds that we're still talking about Charli, Chase, Loren, Baby Ariel, and Avani in the upcoming years might be higher than you think. Plus, every day new people sign up for the app and create new videos, trends, and viral sensations, which means that more and more major stars will start emerging on the platform. And while we have no idea what they might do next, we can always say that we knew them first, before they were big—back when they were just TikTok stars!

WRITE YOUR OWN SCOOP!

It's 2021, and TikTok is bigger than ever. What are the biggest trends going to be?

1 What's the song everyone can't stop dancing to?

_____

_____

2 What's the hot new makeup trend?

_____

_____

3 What's the new #pov meme?

_____

_____

What are the three best TikTok dance trends in your opinion, and why?

1

_____

_____

_____

2

_____

_____

_____

3

_____

_____

_____

Who are the next big stars to emerge on the platform? Someone you love now that you think is about to really explode? Why?

_____

_____

_____

_____

_____

_____

_____

_____

_____

Who are the next big mainstream celebrities to sign up for TikTok and start trying to Renegade? Why?

1. _____
   _____
   _____

2. _____
   _____
   _____

3. _____
   _____
   _____

You get to pick anyone you want to collab with. Who are you working with, and why?

1 _____

_____

_____

2 _____

_____

_____

3 _____

_____

_____

ANSWER KEY

♥ ♥ ♥

STARS WHO STARTED OUT ON SOCIAL MEDIA
1. A. Vine, 2. D. Drake,
3. C. Shawn Mendes, 4. B. Ariana Grande,
5. C. Adele, 6. A Vlogbrothers,
7. C. MySpace, 8. Vine,
9. B. IISUperwomanII, 10. C. Scooter Braun

HOW WELL DO *YOU* KNOW VIRAL TIKTOK AUDIOS?
1. C. Prom dress, 2. A. Conan Gray,
3. B. "The Box", 4. A. *Ice Age*,
5. C. Party all night, 6. C. 24kGoldn,
7. B. Say So, 8. A. "Break My Stride,"
9. D. Kesha, 10. C. John Mulaney

HELP US PICK THE
NEXT ISSUE OF

SCOOP!

HERE'S HOW TO VOTE:

Go to

www.ReadScoop.com

to cast your vote for
who we should
SCOOP! next.